Motivation
For Success

By Adrian Denney

© Copyright 2014 by Adrian Denney

Adrian Denney has asserted his right under the Copyright, Designs and Patents Act, 1988 to be identified as the author of this work.

All rights reserved. No part of this publication may be reproduced, stored in a retrieval system, or transmitted in any form or by any means, electronic, mechanical photocopying, recording or otherwise without the prior permission of the copyright holder.

Published in 2014 by Benbow Publications

British Library
Cataloguing in Publication Data.

ISBN: 978-1-908760-10-4

Printed by Lightning Source UK Ltd
Chapter House
Pitfield
Kiln Farm
Milton Keynes
MK11 3LW

First Edition

A very down to earth realisation of life and its trials and tribulations.
In other words, there is something on every page for every reader, no matter what their outlook on life may be.

A book inspired by an amazing friend of mine who motivated himself despite serious health conditions, which eventually caught up with him.

Glenn Pollard pushed the boundaries of Motivation to the limit and inspired so many people.

This book is dedicated to Glenn who was fondly known as "The King of one Liners".

A percentage of the book sales will go the Brain Tumor Charity.

About the author Adrian Denney

I have been in the IT & retail industry for many years and have been involved with motivating people on a daily basis. Also, being a counsellor for over 30 years it became apparent how much motivation played a part on people finding themselves and finding the strength to move forward in their careers and private lives.

This book is for those that need a touch of reality, humour and inspiration to face the next challenge(s) in their lives.

"A page a day will keep the doctor away."

"Sip and dip through the book" to find the inspiration I found in putting this book together and that of Glenn Pollard, who would read some of these one liners to inspire himself and others who listened.

Don't wait for the green light to do something as you will have lost the moment of opportunity.

Experience is based on failures becoming successful outcomes!

There is always an answer, and you might be staring it in the face, so stop looking in the mirror and get on with it!

Don't follow the signs until you have read them.

A meeting a day will keep the work away!

I am very proud of my achievements; the only problem is I can't remember the last one!

I achieved a high rate of success, then I woke up and remembered all the things I haven't done, so I went back to sleep!

The experience of my achievements is only limited by my retirement.

My job title carries far more importance than my work ethic.

A realistic target may be a moving one if you do not focus on your objective.

My sales figures are a realistic target, so my manager says, but he doesn't have my band of merry non-conformist customers!

My excuses are very well planned and delivered, it's just a shame my targets are not in the same category.

My targets are driven by my enthusiasm.

I never worry about checking my targets, as they are always behind me as I race forward.

I wake up every morning ready to face the challenges in life, and I know I will succeed.

I am the light and soul of the office; it makes up for my poor output.

My waistline is far greater than my sales figures!

The longer in the job, the less I do!

I found I was happy today and then realised I had unexpectedly worked hard for a change.

My knowledge is only limited by my confidence.

I share my knowledge with my colleagues, but only enough so they don't know more than me.

My "must, should, could list" has not been updated for a week, as I only do the things I like to do!

I am a team player well, what I mean is, my name is on the list.

You need light to find your way, so open the shutters in your mind and all will become clear!

Coincidences are an opportunity to realise there is a greater meaning beyond the spoken word.

Have a magnetic personality and draw to you the people who need you.

My motivation is driven by the guilt of not doing my work!

I love talking about my motivation; it's an excuse to not focus on my work.

Motivation is a diary date that keeps reminding you that you have not done your work.

Motivation is a promise that can be a shallow reflection of intention.

I take my work seriously except when I don't value myself.

Three steps to get on in life, work hard, work hard, and work hard – then the work talks for us and not empty promises of fulfilment.

I wanted to get more out of life, until I realised you had to put more in!

My success is your success (Teamwork!).

I don't hold out for hope to make things better, I just keep working through my "Things to do list".

I got up early one morning out of commitment, then realised I was not up for it, so I went back to bed again!

Someone said I want to be like you! What do they know that I don't?

I am serious about my lifestyle and then I realised it was like a pigsty!

Motivation is progress without fear or frustration getting in the way.

I woke up one morning in despair and realised my smartphone had not charged and the commitment of using my own brain was just too much!

I have an 'app' for every possible query on my smartphone, but I can't find one for getting motivated in the morning!

My image is a derivative of the electronic devices I carry or wear!

If my smartphone is charged up for the day, I feel charged up and ready to face the day.

If I have an android phone does it mean that I am an android, or do I just look like one?

I perspire not because I am hot, it's just I think I am on the right pathway, but don't really know and I am looking for some magical sign or word to say that I am!

I need another 10 hours in every day to get my work done, or another 10 hours to worry if I am doing the right thing!

You can lose anything, as we all do at times, but don't lose your mind!

I am trying to lose some weight! It's the wait before I get on with the job.

I love my job, it's just the tasks I don't like!

My idea of teamwork is that the team come up with the ideas and I take the credit for it!

My appearance is the indicator of the state my mind is in! Why advertise madness on the cusp of insanity.

Responsibility has an effect on people. If you are not sure have a look in the mirror!

I am young, attractive and in the prime of my life, it's just a shame I have only discovered this 35 years later!

I like to make fun of myself, so I have a good start on anyone else having a go!

My hairstyle represents how my mind is when the wind of life blows. It looked good once, but looks as if the body had been lived in and the owner had moved out!

I smile with a grimace that is slightly threatening, just in case someone wants to reject my vulnerability.

I am dying to get an appraisal of how my life is going, but I don't want God to give me the appraisal just yet in case I can turn things around!

My image is everything...everything I can find in my wardrobe of lost hope!

Thought is the delay between instinct.

My clothes are a reflection of my disorganised mind!

I love life, so I set a reminder every Tuesday just in case I am too busy and miss the experience!

Honesty is a path that has no edges for you to trip over. The path is smooth so you do not have to look down.

Take courage, not pills

Eat with your mouth and not with your mind!

Hate is a word without meaning. It is a fear of failure. Dislike is not personal.

The drug for life is life. The alternative is the afterlife!

Holding your tongue is as slippery as the words that fall out of your mouth!

A headache is an unresolved conflict, so don't give it to others! Deal with it and the sun will shine.

Pain in the heart is like sitting on a bed of nails. Stop it before it becomes a pain in the backside!

Happiness is walking the pathway and realising how lucky you are.

Walk with purpose even if you do not really know where you are going. Before you know it others will follow you!

Inspiration is the right way. Perspiration is the fear of walking that pathway!

Freedom is not physical movement, but the release of self-perpetual doubt and fear.

Make someone happy today and smile from the heart.

Count your blessings, not the points on your loyalty card.

The future is bright, but why should you have all your surprises at once!

Music can re-ignite the soul, but it is up to you to keep the light going.

Hold onto what you have got. Keep all those precious memories for they are the substance that fills in all the cracks along the pathway of your life!

To discover a lost treasure, look in the mirror.

If your wardrobes and drawers are overflowing with clothes then count your blessings as there are those who still have nothing to put in a wardrobe.

The formula of life is living it. The formula is only complicated if we add to it, then we don't get the right answers…it is called hindsight in this case.

Never worry about the wind messing up your hair as there are many who would wish for such an experience, but, like the rabbit, the hare is long gone!

Achievement is an action that does not accept failure.

Use it or lose it is the reminder that we have wandered off the pathway of life!

Commitment is a direction that never gives you a certification of completion unless you lose your mind.

Fear is trust without confidence.

Never worry if you are not as clever as the next person, for someone already wished the same and it was you they were looking at.

My life has been perfect; it's just my mind that confuses the issue.

Hold onto what you have got before gravity takes over!

To have control you must let it go.

Miracles happen every day. If you are not sure, pinch yourself and realise that you are one of them.

Pack your clothes for your holiday, and if you want a super holiday leave your mind behind!

Sit quietly to find yourself. Some travel all over the world and still don't find themselves.

As the years went on I put on more weight. I am still holding onto things!

An effort is something we do without willingness!

Give 100% each day and you will find resistance is only from the mind.

Change is the bitter pill of success!

Be honest, for truth is the key to happiness.

Happiness is a commitment to please.

If you do not want to fear, look beyond yourself.

I felt better today because I didn't start with worrying, I just fretted a little!

I felt someone staring at me today and I felt uncomfortable, so I looked away from the mirror. What is your reflection saying?

When I was a child I spoke like a child. When I grew up I did the same. Where did I go wrong?

Write your truths in your heart for there are no laptops in heaven!

If I have gained weight without reason maybe I am trying to hide inside?

My wealth is my stealth, or is it?

To hold onto your worries hold your breath and when you have to grasp for air again let them go. Worries should only be passing thoughts without delay.

Love, and when you cannot love, rest, and the work will continue the next day.

My mind is like the wind as it is forever changing. Unfortunately, the hurricane of thoughts has left me desolate. My mind must be more powerful than I thought! Let's hope next time it is a summer breeze.

I am body perfect on the inside, it's just the body tucks from the inside that are showing on the outside.

My mobile tariff is killing me, but I must have it to keep in touch with my alter ego.

I got up early one morning and then went back to bed as I didn't have a purpose.

I hope to have a long life, but a long life without purpose is like waiting for the bus that never comes.

My face is my destiny. Quick, call a plastic surgeon.

My pathway is full of love and light, it's only my fear of change that holds me back from enjoying the journey.

Experience can be a pain, but not learning from them is even more painful than the reality of life and the acceptance of responsibility.

We carry the responsibilities of our actions. Some of thought and some that contain calories!

When you look at someone, do you look or give?

So you drive a fast and fancy car? Does that really mean you know where you are going?

Money is not the root of all evil, but the intention of how and why it is given is important.

Greatness is not what you think you are, but what others do.

Contemplation is good, but water that stands for too long becomes stagnant.

I don't like my picture taken. I have problems coping with reality.

Empty barrels make the most noise. I stopped talking and the world was quiet again.

I am so happy I could burst. Must be time for another diet.

Today I was persecuted and I did not recognise this person until I looked in the mirror!

My doctor said my condition is life threatening, he said unless you change your attitude others could suffer.

My smartphone is run by an android...it's me!

My boss told me I was useless in an email, dictated and sent by his PA.

I hope for hope that I can cope with the challenges each day. I found this note, does it belong to you?

Trust is a funny thing; I have it until I have a crisis!

Change is a good thing. Try telling my mind that!

The greatest weight to bear is the weight of your thoughts!

I inspire others. They look at me and quietly say to others, "Thank God I am not like that."

A fake tan causes a personality peel.

I have more gadgets than James Bond, so why do I spend my life having to recharge my personality?

I bought a fancy watch the other day, and then I realised my watch had more personality than I did!

I hope one day that I will be forgotten, but remembered by those I gave hope to.

I used to give in, but I learnt to give out.

I met many people covered in bling, but they never made my heart sing. For true light is not an accessory.

I look for rewards in life, but only through the achievements of others.

Miracles are selfless thoughts in a society of selfish progression.

Time has no meaning without purpose.

Write your truths in your heart for there are no laptops in heaven!

If I have gained weight without reason maybe I am trying to hide inside?

My wealth is my stealth, or is it?

To hold onto your worries hold your breath and when you have to grasp for air again let them go. Worries should only be passing thoughts without delay.

Love, and when you cannot love, rest, and the work will continue the next day.

My mind is like the wind as it is forever changing. Unfortunately, the hurricane of thoughts has left me desolate. My mind must be more powerful than I thought! Let's hope next time it is a summer breeze.

I am body perfect on the inside, it's just the body tucks from the inside that are showing on the outside.

My mind is a state...a state of standby and service, and time becomes my friend and not my enemy.

I used to have a friend that was really silly and got on people's nerves. I asked him to leave one day and found it was my alter ego!

The wise ones are seen, but often not seen for who they are.

A life cycle is good. A pedal cycle is even better.

I dress to impress just in case someone sees through my disguise!

Thousands of people are dying of obesity, while millions are dying of the thought of it.

I often find myself laughing at myself. I only told you this before you started!

I am nobody's fool; I got the title by my own effort!

Experience is knowing you shouldn't have done it, but intuition does not come with an override button!

Others constantly make mistakes; it's just my persistence that carries me through.

I am the most interesting person you could ever meet, it's just that I am too humble to bore you with my success.

Speech is for teaching and inspiring and not for recreating your fears in others.

I find it difficult to express my feelings, so I put others down, just in case they really tell me what I already know!

I have problems picking things off the floor as I have a bad back, but I often put my foot in my mouth.

Truth can be a most welcome friend, or a reality check on your perceived personality.

My IQ is so high I have forgotten what IQ really means!

I am gracious and loving. I am kind and appreciated. I forgive myself, but don't expect me to do it for others, as my perception of myself is supporting my ego.

I would have a wonderful life, if God hadn't give me such an awful disability...my mind!

I am in two minds, one belongs to my boss and the other I don't know how to use unless given permission to use it!

The best gems in the world are the ones that you find in the eyes of the ones you love and respect.

If you are a friend to yourself then you welcome others as friends, yet there are so many who are not a friend to themselves, who cannot see beyond their fears.

Charity is not a giving of reluctance, but a giving beyond one's own necessity of existence.

Prosperity is only a pleasure if it is shared, otherwise it's an indulgence.

I used to have a fit body, now my body is fit for a refit, time for change I think!

We pay great attention to our financial matters will mature, yet we often forget to do the same for our children.

I listen to others in the hope I can say something to impress them with my wit and intelligence, yet there are others who listen for the right reasons.

If you fail in a task, then you have tried. If you ignore the task then you have failed!

To be tolerant of others, you have to be tolerant of yourself.

I had indigestion one day, and I realised it was nothing to do with what I ate, but the indecision in my mind. Fear is the best laxative for those blocked thoughts, but please do not go there!

If someone borrowed your car and misused it you would be very upset, so why do the same to your body!

If your mind carries too many thoughts it will slow you down, and if you load your body with more sustenance than you need this too will have the same effect.

No one rocks your boat, as you are the captain who will steer the boat away from the storms of life.

If your PC slows down, re-boot it. If your mind does the same, sit in isolation and meditate for a while and all will be well.

An active mind is a positive thing, an over active mind will confuse the owner.

Control your mind before it controls you!

The greatest strength is not your body but your mind. Use that strength wisely for without regulation it will defeat you as if it does not belong to you.

Take heart in all that you do. For positive upliftment compensates for the little knocks in life.

My heart hurts not because of exercise, but the emotional battering I give it.

Weight a moment, a calorie is calling me.

My life is full of meaning. I am mean to everyone including myself.

I have no enemies compared to the insults I give myself.

What a wonderful world this is. The only problem, my mind will not let me enjoy it.

I hate to lose. The problem is I am racing myself and I still cannot win.

If you are looking for surprises in your life don't look for them, earn them.

My life is full of surprises, but I have to check with my partner that I am allowed to enjoy them!

We have been married for 38 years and I could not be happier, but you'll have to ask my wife yourself as she is not speaking to me. *Relationship is not just a word.*

Enjoy the food for it is there to sustain the body and not to strain the robes you wear.

It is better to have doubt before an action, rather than regret afterwards.

You may lose your data on your PC. Better this than lose your mind.

Make your mind up, before someone does it for you!

Persistence pays off, resistance doesn't.

Giving out is far better than giving in.

Take heed, not tablets.

I walk with a swagger to show how important I think I am.

Opportunities fall into two categories, those that you accepted and those that will come your way again. So why fight it!

Love does not come easily. You have to give it away before you get it.

Out of sight becomes insight with intuitive thought.

If you become impatient, you will end up as a patient!

Health is too late when you leave it to the hospitals then blaming them for poor service!

Before you blame someone else, blame yourself if you can. For we all have faults of thought or deed.

Being human is part of the plan for man.

Trust is not conditional, it is instinctive without reason.

A dentist may hit a nerve, but how often do you do the same to others.

Hate is only a fear of self-failure.

Success is the only answer that we need.

You talk how you walk.

Speak without an image.

Look to help, not for recognition.

Be inspired by others, in the knowledge that they may be inspired by you!

If you are reading this book you are privileged, for so many would have loved the opportunity to learn to read.

Give in to giving; it is the only way forward.

How wonderful conscious free thought is, so take the time to exercise it beyond your fears.

If you want to find someone who speaks words of wisdom and will guide you, listen to your soul.

Don't be afraid to talk to strangers. The only stranger is yourself, so once you make friends with yourself, talking to others is easy!

Hope is for those who are not determined to succeed.

Life is for trying, but remember don't be trying with others!

Fear is only an option in life, better live without it than die with it.

If I exercised my body as much as I exercise my mind, then I would have the six pack and not the party 7 keg!

My body is fit now, but my mind is fit for a refit!

Some people lift weights to keep fit, others carry them around in their mind!

Rest is good when you have completed a task, but not if there is no reason.

Allow your eyes to connect to your soul and you will rescue many who have eyes and are frightened to use them!

Light up someone's world with unconditional love and you will not need words.

My face is my fortune. That is why I am broke! What's your excuse?

I thought being happy was having lots of money to solve all my problems, but I realised it's the state of my emotions that count and not the state of my bank account.

A business plan starts with yourself and not with the company!

I love being happy. It confuses so many who have everything and then realise they are missing that special ingredient...love!

I used to live in fear. It's quite easy to find. Turn left, left again, once more left and you will find yourself again.

I am instinctive. I know when someone doesn't like me, because I didn't like me before they ever did!

I have gained years of experience, and I am accumulating most of it on my waistline!

I used to wake up worrying. I then used to worry about not waking up. I realise the first option is the best!

Failure only means PRESS RESET and have another go!

The challenges in life start with you and end with you. Don't give away perfect opportunities to grow, for we are stronger than we think.

My doctor said there was nothing wrong with me. *I said if you could only look in my mind!*

I laughed so much today, I forgot who I am. What a pleasant interlude that was!

A challenge is an opportunity to prove your strength for others.

My partner said 'you inspire me'. I felt good and then realised, they meant not to be like that!

My eyes see what I am feeling, so make the experience a film worth watching.

I live in my earphones, to stop me hearing the cries of help from others.

I have no regrets, just experiences!

Put hope in yourself, before you try it with others.

I like myself, I accept myself, but don't ask me to prove it!

If you want an uplifting day, carry someone else.

My face is a result of my living inside of me!

The furrows on my brow are there for the seeds of discontentment I keep planting. Time for some weeding!

A mind is a terrible thing and can be the worst disability, as nobody can see the pain we put ourselves through. Why not let go, to let in!

Is it time for a New Year's resolution or time to let go of last year's resolution?

Great work needs great minds, open and ready to be inspired. Is yours open or awaiting refurbishment?

Start each day with a healthy appetite for living.

Take great care of yourself, before someone who does not know you has to!

I am only wrong in other people's eyes.

Count your blessings and not the wrinkles on your forehead.

There is no such thing as luck but an opportunity to share.

I am full of energy and ready for the challenges ahead, the only problem is I am too comfortable in bed.

My face tells a story which is full of life's experience and the struggle to face another day - and that was only from yesterday.

I check my watch just in case I am late for an appointment I have not made!

Life is only confusing if you concentrate on the journey and not the meaning of the journey.

I know I am right, for my ego tells me so!

Money is not the answer to all our problems, for what you cannot hold in your heart will never be enough.

My voice is an instrument of inspiration unless fear is my topic of the day!

People are often so busy these days they don't even know where they are going. Why not pick a destination and then start your journey for you will achieve far more if the journey involves others.

I hated going to school, until I realised there were so many who hated not having the chance.

I dislike change so much, so when opportunity comes my way I grab it with both hands and push the changes out the way!

I know how to do my job for I have learnt the procedures and practices, if only I could do the same with my life, but the problem is I don't like responsibility.

The sun shines every day somewhere in the world. Do you?

You may have a sat-nav, but it still may mean you don't know where you are going in life!

Makeup may cover your face but don't let it cover your personality!

Learn to be excited with life, as the alternative is days that have more than 24 hours in them and the nights are even longer!

Lust is a must that is a perfume people chase and realise it does not smell as good when they get it!

Tone and shape your body and you will look good, but don't forget to do the same with your mind, as shop dummies are full of plastic and not personality.

Live with emotion not in fear of it!

Smiles last longer than money does.

Hate is fate for all who hold it.

Light travels faster than the speed of sound, but my fears are even quicker!

Don't speak to me this morning, as I have had a row with myself!

I drive a fast car because my fear keeps catching me up.

Today do I face the challenges in front of me or face the challenges I create?

Do you have a spring in your step, or is that emotional baggage becoming that heavy?

The dustman calls once a week to empty your rubbish, how often do you empty yours from your head!

I don't often smile just in case people see me!

A drain inspector will look down. Are you a drain inspector?

Live in the fast lane for too long and you will be at your destination before you realise it!

Experience can be a comfort, so make it the right sort of experience.

Be loved for your qualities and not the acceptance of your fears.

Take pride, not prisoners!

Remove grudges like smudges.

Are you full of beans today, or just full of caffeine!

Do not be influenced by the noise of life, as distraction is no excuse for getting on with the things that we do.

A task is to be finished, not to be an open door of excuses.

There is always a way out of a situation, it just needs the most positive energy you have.

Achievement means action. Try it you may like it.

If you want to get ahead in life, loose the fear.

The Internet is no substitute for inspiration and hard work, unless we use it with meaning.

A smartphone does not mean the user fits in the same category!

Be inspired before you are expired.

Love the challenges in life, but please do learn from them!

If you love yourself then you will see everyone else in the same light.

Hope is a short piece of rope going nowhere, belief is a path with endless opportunities.

Designer clothes and designer smiles have no miles, they are blind to anything spiritual, for they do not look for their Gods as they already think they are iconic in their own mind.

Confusion means you have engaged a reaction without understanding the purpose of the direction you are taking.

Give with your heart and not your mouth!

Wisdom is a smile from the heart.

Success is a positive result, derived from a positive action.

Health is peace combined with living life and enjoying the journey.

There is always a solution to a problem if fear is not factored in.

Thoughts are positive or negative actions, the choice is yours, so karma can be your friend if you wish.

I don't like four letter words.... fear, hate, pain.

I carried extra weight most of my life and then I realised it was all in my mind.

Someone read my mind once. They are still recovering and I visit them twice a week. Powerful stuff the mind!

If you have a gift share it. I did. Now I have loads of friends as I had a gift for loving and accepting myself! The rest was easy.

I am obsessed by special offers like "buy one and get one free". I now do this with friendship and I have never looked back.

If you want to feel guilty, only feel guilty for not loving and accepting yourself before.

Write words from your heart, not from your dictionary of acceptable phrases

I am a child at heart. All I need is love.

Friendship is not an accessory or a "bolt on." It's the most precious thing whether it's family or not.

A journey is much more satisfying if you take in the sights rather than just focus on the destination.

This could be the best day of your life or your last! If you knew which one, would you live it any differently?

A smile is seen long after the words are not heard.

Reach out and touch someone before there is a law against it!

If your bottom hurts sitting on a seat, maybe you have sat for too long!

The next time you need inspiration read from the book, or put pen to paper and write some yourself, as you are more than capable of doing this too.

Read and share as I have done and I wish you well.

If you have reached the end of the book, you have only just started the journey of self-discovery.

Lightning Source UK Ltd.
Milton Keynes UK
UKOW06f0026020514

230968UK00006B/8/P